Get Art Smart

What Is Line?

by Susan Markowitz Meredith

Crabtree Publishing Company
www.crabtreebooks.com

Crabtree Publishing Company

Author: Susan Meredith
Publishing plan research and development:
    Sean Charlebois, Reagan Miller
    Crabtree Publishing Company
Editors: Reagan Miller
Proofreader: Kathy Middleton, Molly Aloian
Editorial director: Kathy Middleton
Photo research: Edward A. Thomas
Designer: Tammy West, Westgraphix LLC
Production coordinator: Margaret Amy Salter
Prepress technician: Margaret Amy Salter
Consultant: Julie Collins-Dutkiewicz, B.A., specialist in early
    childhood education, Sandy Waite, M.Ed., U.S. National
    Board Certified Teacher, author, and literacy consultant
Reading Consultant: Susan Nations, M.Ed.,
Author/Literacy Coach/Consultant in Literacy Development

Photographs and reproductions
Cover: iStock; 1: Adobe Image Library; 5, 13: Private
Collection/The Bridgeman Art Library; 9: Private Collection/The
Stapleton Collection/The Bridgeman Art Library; 11: Tokyo Fuji
Art Museum, Tokyo, Japan/The Bridgeman Art Library; 15:
Phillips Collection, Washington, D.C./The Bridgeman Art Library;
17: FuZhai Archive/The Bridgeman Art Library; 19: Fitzwilliam
Museum, University of Cambridge, UK/The Bridgeman Art
Library; 21: Bibliotheque Nationale, Paris/Lauros/Giraudon/
The Bridgeman Art Library; 23: Family of Lawren S. Harris/
Art Gallery of Ontario, Toronto/The Bridgeman Art Library.

Front cover (main image): A young artist is excited at the line possibilities.
Title page: A young girl uses a marker to make lines, in her coloring book.
Written, developed, and produced by RJF Publishing LLC

Library and Archives Canada Cataloguing in Publication

Meredith, Susan, 1951-
    What is line? / Susan Markowitz Meredith.

(Get art smart)
Includes index.
ISBN 978-0-7787-5122-9 (bound).--ISBN 978-0-7787-5136-6 (pbk.)

    1. Line (Art)--Juvenile literature. I. Title. II. Series: Get art smart

N7430.5.M47 2009   j701'.8   C2009-903588-X

Library of Congress Cataloging-in-Publication Data

Meredith, Susan, 1951-
    What is line? / Susan Markowitz Meredith.
      p. cm. -- (Get art smart)
    Includes index.
    ISBN 978-0-7787-5136-6 (pbk. : alk. paper) -- ISBN 978-0-7787-5122-9 (re-
inforced library binding : alk. paper)
    1. Line (Art)--Juvenile literature. I. Title. II. Series.

N7430.5.M47 200
701'.8--dc22

2009022912

Crabtree Publishing Company

www.crabtreebooks.com   1-800-387-7650

**Published
in Canada
Crabtree Publishing**
616 Welland Ave.
St. Catharines, Ontario
L2M 5V6

**Published in
the United States
Crabtree Publishing**
PMB16A
350 Fifth Ave., Suite 3308
New York, NY 10118

**Published in the
United Kingdom
Crabtree Publishing**
Maritime House
Basin Road North, Hove
BN41 1WR

**Published
in Australia
Crabtree Publishing**
386 Mt. Alexander Rd.
Ascot Vale (Melbourne)
VIC 3032

Contents

What Is a Line? 4

Lines of All Kinds 6

Lines in Art 8

Using Different Sizes 10

This Way and That 12

Lines Show Texture 14

Making Patterns 16

Lines That Move 18

Showing Feelings 20

Lines Help Artists 22

Words to Know and Find Out More 24

Look at the mark shown below:

It is called a **line**. Some lines are short, and some are long. Some lines are **thin**, and some are **thick**. Lines can show us the **outline** of a shape. An outline is the line around a shape.

Can you find long lines, short lines, thin lines, and thick lines in this painting?

Linear Construction, by Lyubov Sergeevna Popova (1921)

5

Lines of All Kinds

There are many kinds of lines. We can make straight lines and curved lines. We can make wavy lines and zigzag lines, too. Sometimes we can make one big line out of many small dashes. This is called a broken line.

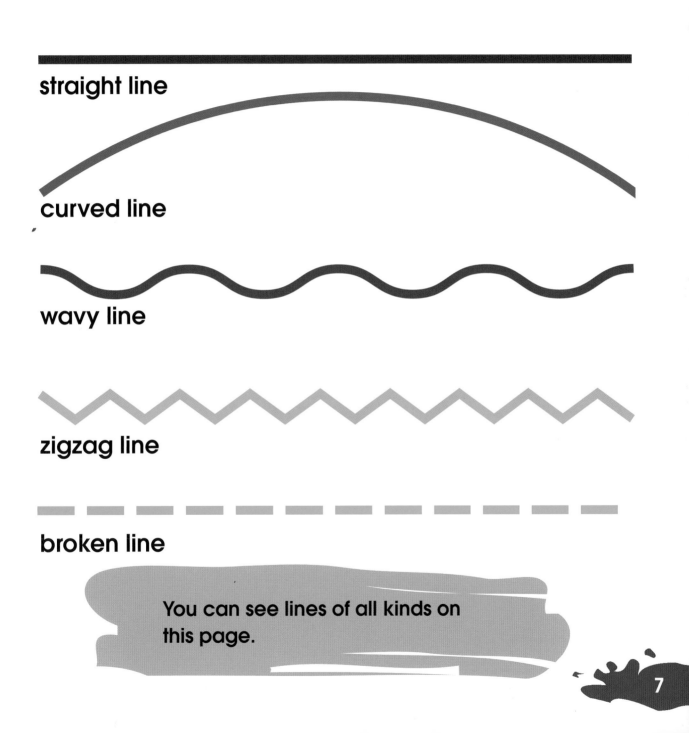

straight line

curved line

wavy line

zigzag line

broken line

You can see lines of all kinds on this page.

Lines in Art

We can use lines in different ways when we make art. Sometimes a line is used alone. Sometimes a group of lines are next to each other. We can also make shapes with lines.

8

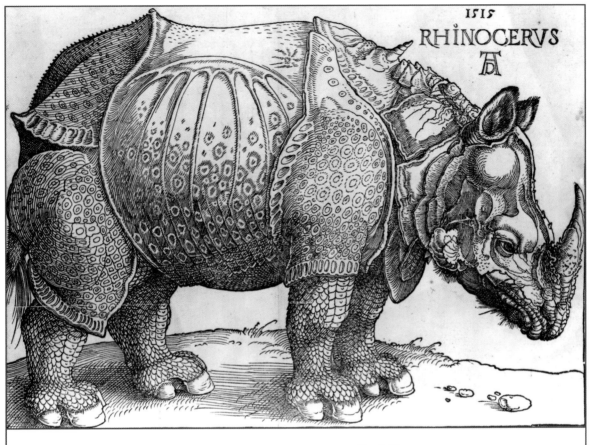

Rhinoceros engraving, by Albrecht Durer (1515)

The artist used lines to make the shape of a rhinoceros.

Using Different Sizes

We can use both thin and thick lines when we make art. Sometimes we can change the size of a line. It may start out thick and then get thinner.

The Cherry Garden at Kameido,
by Ando Hiroshige (1856)

The artist used
thin lines and
thick lines
to make a
cherry tree.

This Way and That

We can make lines go this way and that. Some lines go straight up and down. Some lines go from side to side across the paper. Other lines go uphill or downhill. These are slanted, or **diagonal**, lines.

12

View of Malakoff, Hauts-de-Seine, by Henri Rousseau (1908)

Look at the street. It is made with diagonal lines. What other kinds of lines can you find?

Lines Show Texture

We can use lines to do many things. Sometimes lines can show an object's **texture**. Texture is how an object looks and feels. Objects may look smooth or rough. They may seem hard or soft, too.

The Road Menders, by Vincent van Gogh (1889)

The artist used lines to make the tree trunks look rough in this painting.

Making Patterns

We can make patterns with the lines we use in art. In a picture of a room, we can use lines to put a pattern on a wall. In another picture, we can use lines to add patterns to people's clothes. We can use patterns in many kinds of artwork.

The Cocoon Stage, by Kitagawa Utamaro (1800)

Can you find patterns in the women's clothes?

17

Lines That Move

We can use lines to make it look like something is moving. It may be an animal running. It may be a person stretching or dancing.

Dancers in Violet Dresses, Arms Raised,
by Edgar Degas (1900)

In this picture, the artist used lines to show the dancers raising their arms.

We can use lines to show different feelings, too. Lines can show that someone is happy or sad. Sometimes we can use just a few lines to show a feeling.

La Potion, Draught, by Honore Daumier (1836)

Look at the woman's face. Lines show us how she feels about taking medicine.

Lines Help Artists

Lines are very helpful when we make art. Different lines can make a texture or show something moving. Lines may be straight, thin, and diagonal. They may be thick and wavy. Lines can be anything we want. Every line helps make an artwork special. How do you use lines?

Above Lake Superior, by Lawren S. Harris (1922)

There are many kinds of lines in this picture.
What kinds of lines do you see?

Words to Know

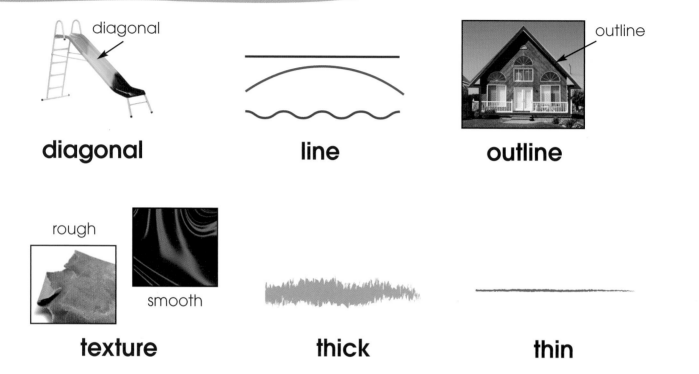

diagonal

line

outline

rough

smooth

texture

thick

thin

Find Out More

Books

Gibson, Ray. *I Can Draw People*. New York: Random House, 2000.

Tougas, Chris. *Art's Supplies*. Custer, WA: Orca Book Publishers, 2008.

Web sites

Art Pad
artpad.art.com/artpad/painter/

The Artist's Toolkit—Line
www.artsconnected.org/toolkit/watch_types_line.cfm

Printed in the USA—CG